MW00630334

CRIME AND PUNISHMENT

by
Fyodor Dostoevsky

Translated by
Constance Garnett

Teacher Guide

Written by
Pat Watson

Edited by
Monica L. Odle

Note

The Bantam Classic, a division of Doubleday Dell Publishing, Inc., paperback edition of the book, ©1958, 1981, was used to prepare this guide. The page references may differ in other editions.

Please note: This novel deals with sensitive, mature issues. Parts may contain profanity, sexual references, and/or descriptions of violence. Please assess the appropriateness of this book for the age level and maturity of your students prior to reading and discussing it with them.

ISBN 1-58130-802-7

To order, contact your local school supply store, or—
Novel Units, Inc.
P.O. Box 97
Bulverde, TX 78163-0097

Web site: www.educyberstor.com

Table of Contents

Skills and Strategies

Comprehension
Cause/effect,
prediction, summarization

Writing
Poetry, newspaper article,
opinion essay, resume,
eulogy

Literary Elements
Characterization, theme,
mood, tone, simile,
metaphor, allusion, inference,
irony, sequence

Thinking
Analysis, compare/
contrast, research

Vocabulary
Target words, definitions,
application

Listening/Speaking
Discussion, interview,
oral presentation

Across the Curriculum
Art—collage, poster;
Drama—script; Music—
appropriate selection;
Current Events—articles,
pictures; Multi-media—slide
show, video presentation

Genre: fiction

Setting: St. Petersburg, Russia; a prison in Siberia; 1860s

Date of First Publication: 1866

Point of View: third-person omniscient

Style: narrative

Themes: the human condition, e.g., guilt, conscience, alienation, pride, suffering, sacrifice; family relationships; nihilism; fate/chance; redemption/resurrection; social order, e.g., scientific vs. traditional values, gender, social class

Conflict: person vs. self; person vs. person; person vs. society

Mood: fatalistic, tragic

Tone: solemn, ironic

Summary

Rodion Romanovitch Raskolnikov, a young, destitute former student in St. Petersburg, Russia, plots and carries out a plan to murder a detestable pawnbroker—an unloved old woman. In his own mind, he justifies the murder because he feels superior to other humans and believes he can transgress moral law because he is ridding humanity of a "louse." In the course of carrying out his plan, he also murders the pawnbroker's sister, an innocent victim. Unable to face the enormity of his crime, he begins a psychological journey into guilt and torment. He eventually confesses and is sentenced to eight years in a Siberian prison. Sonia, a young woman who had been forced into prostitution because of her family's poverty, guides Raskolnikov on a gradual path to redemption. She follows him to Siberia, and their love for each other sustains them as they anticipate a happy future.

Characters

Raskolnikov (Rodya): 23-year-old protagonist; intelligent, handsome, impoverished former student; commits murder (the crime) and lives in psychological terror and alienation (the punishment)

Dounia: Raskolnikov's sister; intelligent, compassionate; willing to marry a wealthy man she does not love to help her mother and brother

Pulcheria Alexandrovna Raskolnikov: Raskolnikov's mother; devoted to her son; willing to sacrifice Dounia's happiness for him; unable to accept his guilt

Alyona Ivanovna: the miserly pawnbroker; murder victim

Lizaveta Ivanovna: Alyona's subservient sister; murder victim

Marmeladov: self-deprecating former public official whom Raskolnikov meets in a tavern; knows his alcoholism is destroying his family but is unable to stop

Katerina Ivanovna: Marmeladov's wife who is dying from consumption; proud of her aristocratic heritage

Sonia: Marmeladov's frail, lovely teenage daughter; deeply religious; becomes a prostitute to save her family from starving to death; aids Raskolnikov in his search for redemption

Nastasya Petrovna: cook and servant of Raskolnikov's landlady; cares for Raskolnikov when he is ill

Razumihin: Raskolnikov's kind, amiable friend; advises and protects Dounia and her mother

Pyotr Petrovitch Luzhin: Dounia's miserly, self-centered fiancé

Svidrigaïlov: Dounia's debauched former employer with a questionable past; overhears Raskolnikov's confession to Sonia; attempts to seduce Dounia

Zossimov: doctor who treats Raskolnikov during his illness

Ilya Petrovitch: explosive assistant superintendent of police to whom Raskolnikov eventually confesses

Zametov: assistant police clerk; suspects Raskolnikov

Nikodim Fomitch: police captain

Porfiry Petrovitch: head of Investigation Department; Raskolnikov's primary antagonist

Nikolay: painter who confesses to the murders

Lebeziatnikov: young man with whom Luzhin is staying; expounds philosophy of nihilism

Background Information

1. **Tsar Nicholas I:** ruler of Russia from 1825–1855; removed aristocrats from government office and replaced them with professional military officers; tightened government control of the press and education; prohibited organizations that might have political influence

2. **Siberia:** a thinly populated region making up 75% of the area of Russia with only 20% of the population living there; covered by ice and snow about 6 months of the year, with temperatures dropping to -90°F. Through the centuries, millions of political and criminal prisoners have been sent to prisons in isolated parts of Siberia.

3. **Karl Marx (Introduction, p. v):** German philosopher and economist; one of the most influential socialist leaders; wrote *Communist Manifesto* in 1848

4. **Socialism:** a system in which the primary means of production and distribution are owned, managed, or controlled by the government

5. **People's Commissars (p. v):** heads of government departments in Russia

6. **Utopian Socialist (p. xv):** an extreme, visionary idealist who believes socialism will affect an ideal society with justice and equality for all citizens

7. **Utilitarianism (p. xvi):** theory of morality that associates the rightness of an act with its consequences, i.e., actions are good if they are useful; expounds on the idea that providing the greatest good for the greatest number should be the purpose of human conduct

8. **Nihilism (p. xvii):** from Latin word meaning "nothing;" rejection of established beliefs, e.g., religious, moral, governmental; belief that no absolute values exist; theory advocating the destruction of the old order by violence to make way for reform in Russia in mid-1800s

9. **Bolshevik Revolution (p. xxii):** November 1917; led to founding of a Communist dictatorship in Russia; a Bolshevik is a member of the Communist Party

About the Author

Fyodor Mikhailovich Dostoevsky was born in Moscow on October 30, 1821. He graduated from the School of Military Engineering at St. Petersburg in 1843 as a sub-lieutenant but left the military to devote himself to writing. His first major work, *Poor Folk*, was published in 1846. In 1849, he was arrested and imprisoned for alleged subversion against the Tsar. He was ordered to face the firing squad; however, just minutes before his death, the Tsar commuted his sentence to exile in a Siberian prison, where he spent four years at hard labor. Dostoevsky depicts his prison experiences in *Memories of the House of the Dead* (1853). He married Marya Isaiev in 1856; she died seven years later. In 1867, he married Anna Snitkina, who helped him attain stability amidst the havoc his compulsive gambling had created. His other works include *The Idiot* (1868–69), *The Possessed* (1871–72), and *The Brothers Karamazov* (1879–80). He contributed "An Author's Note-book" to magazines. Through this and other writings, he gained popular notoriety before his death in February of 1881.

Initiating Activities

1. Brainstorm with students about their prior knowledge of the book. Discuss the title, the cover, the author, when the book was written, and the number of pages in the book. Read aloud one page from the beginning of the book, one near the middle, and one near the end, and then have students make a prediction about the book.

2. Place the word "Guilt" in the center of an overhead transparency. Brainstorm with students causes, reactions, results if not confessed, results if confessed, and remedies.

3. Place the following quote on an overhead transparency and elicit oral student response. "There is no witness so dreadful, no accuser so terrible as the conscience that dwells in the heart of every man." (Polybius, *History*, bk. X, 36; quoted by John Bartlett in *Bartlett's Familiar Quotations*, Sixteenth Edition [Boston: Little, Brown and Company, 85])

4. Summarize the Introduction of the book and present material from the Background Information section in this guide.

5. Discuss Dostoevsky's life history and how his own life experiences influenced his written works.

Foreshadowing Chart

Foreshadowing is the literary technique of giving clues to coming events in a story.

Directions: Think about *Crime and Punishment.* What examples of foreshadowing do you recall from the story? If necessary, skim through the chapters to find examples of foreshadowing. List at least four examples below. Explain what clues are given, then list the coming event that is being suggested.

Foreshadowing	Page #	Clues	Coming Event

Character Chart

Directions: In the rows for each listed feeling, describe an incident or time in the book when each character experienced that feeling. You may use "not applicable" if you cannot find an example. Then write a sixth feeling in the last row and respond to it.

	Raskolnikov	Sonia	Dounia	Razumihin
Frustration				
Anger				
Fear				
Humiliation				
Relief				

Characters With Character

Directions: A person's **character** is evaluated by his or her actions, statements, and by the way he or she treats others. For each of the attributes listed in the center of the page, write the name of one character from the novel who has that trait and the name of a character who does **not** have that trait. After each character's name, give an example of an action or statement that proves you have properly evaluated the character.

Has This Trait		Doesn't Have This Trait
	tells the truth	
	keeps promises	
	considers consequences of actions	
	sacrifices for others	
	listens to others without pre-judging them	
	is a good person	
	is kind and caring	

Story Map

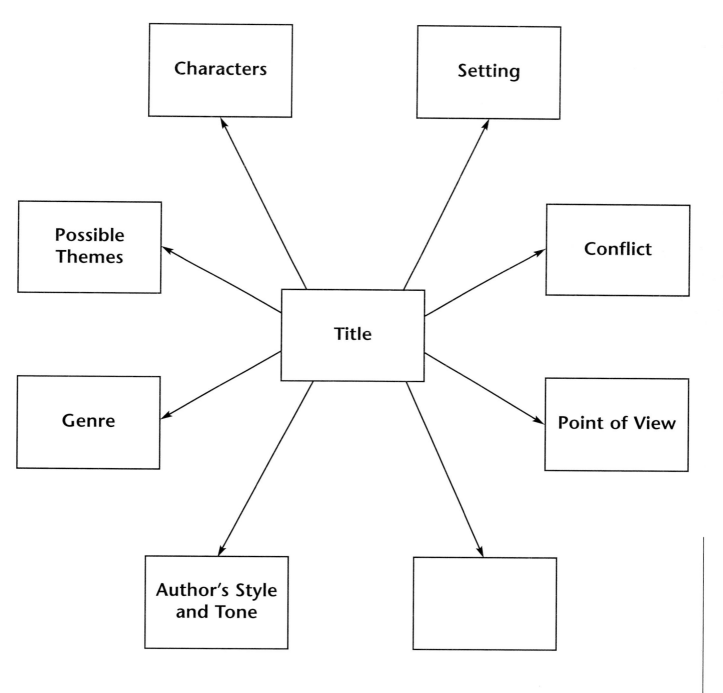

Persuasive Writing Worksheet

Topic (prompt) _____

_____

Points you find for the proposal (pro)	**Points you find against the proposal** (con)
_____	_____
_____	_____
_____	_____
_____	_____

Your choice _____

Thesis (your opinion summarized in one arguable statement) _____

_____

Format

Introduction: Address Audience (Dear...)

Paragraph 2: Effective transition; give reason #1; explain.

Paragraph 3: Effective transition; give reason #2; explain.

Paragraph 4: Effective transition; give reason #3; explain.

Conclusion: Restate prompt; persuade audience.

Checklist for persuasive writing

____1. Does your first paragraph grab the reader's attention?

____2. Are your supporting points clearly stated with adequate elaboration?

____3. Have you presented your arguments in a logical order?

____4. Does your proposal contain any fallacies?

____5. Does each paragraph have unity?

____6. Have you used unifying transitions between paragraphs?

____7. Does your concluding paragraph clinch your position?

Note: Examples of similes and metaphors found in each section are included in the Supplementary Activities. Guide students to identify these devices as they read the novel. In addition, Dostoevsky employs allusions throughout the novel. These are identified at the beginning of each applicable section.

Part I, Chapters I–II, pp. 1–25

Raskolnikov experiences mental conflict as he contemplates his "project" and visits the pawnbroker. He meets Marmeladov, who introduces him to Sonia and Katerina Ivanovna.

Allusions: yellow passport or ticket (p. 12)—a passport identifying a person as a prostitute; Bedlam (p. 15)—place of noise and confusion, an asylum for the mentally ill in London where people paid to watch patients on exhibit (as in a zoo)

Vocabulary
axiom (2)
languid (11)
magnanimous (13)
consumption (13)

Discussion Questions

1. Discuss Raskolnikov and his actions as he first appears in the novel. Analyze his thoughts about his "project" and note the significance of the setting. (*At first he is identified only as a young man. He is self-absorbed and isolated from everyone. He is crushed by poverty, handsome but shabbily dressed, and hopelessly in debt. He lives near the Hay Market, the poor section of St. Petersburg that is filled with establishments of ill repute. The heat and smell emanating from this area add to his nervousness. His purpose on this particular day is to rehearse "it," a project that fills him with great fear and doubts as to his ability to complete it. pp. 1–4*)

2. Discuss Raskolnikov's visit to Alyona Ivanovna and examine what their interaction reveals about both of them. Note what the cigarette case foreshadows. (*She is a withered-up, miserly, severe old pawnbroker whom Raskolnikov has visited before. He probes into whether or not she is usually at home alone or with her sister, Lizaveta. He notes her actions, e.g., her keys, and procedure of getting money for his pawn. He alludes to bringing her a silver cigarette box to pawn, foreshadowing his ploy to return. pp. 4–7*)

3. Examine Raskolnikov's state of mind when he leaves the pawnbroker and the symbolism of his ensuing actions. Note that the author has not yet revealed the exact nature of the project. (*He is confused and engages in a mental battle where he is repulsed by thoughts of committing such a loathsome act and yet is convinced he must do so. For the first time in his life, he enters a tavern and orders a beer, which he believes clears his mind. His descent into the tavern symbolizes the beginning of a physical, mental, and spiritual downward spiral. pp. 7–9*)

4. Discuss Raskolnikov's chance meeting with Marmeladov. (*Raskolnikov is drawn to Marmeladov, who is drinking in the tavern, and believes their meeting is a product of destiny. Marmeladov introduces himself, and their ensuing conversation reveals circumstances of Marmeladov's life. He has lost his job as a government clerk because of his alcoholism, causing his wife and children to live in deep poverty, and his daughter Sonia has become a prostitute to provide money for the family. His wife, Katerina, suffers from consumption. She is an educated and refined woman who does not love him and married him after the death of her first husband only because of her extreme poverty. He tells Raskolnikov that Katerina has a noble heart but also reveals that she is irritable and short-tempered and unjustly beats the children. Marmeladov invites Raskolnikov home with him. After observing the extreme poverty and chaotic living conditions, Raskolnikov leaves his only money for the Marmeladov family, yet he wants to go back and get it. This section introduces the subplot involving the Marmeladov family. pp. 9–25*)

5. Discuss the introduction of the theme of science versus humanity during Raskolnikov's discussion with Marmeladov in the tavern. Continue to look for evidence of this theme throughout the novel. Discuss what personal message Dostoevsky is embedding in his work regarding these ideas. (*Marmeladov refers to Mr. Lebeziatnikov, who will appear later in the novel, and who believes in "modern" ideologies and asserts that compassion is not allowed by science. Discussions will vary but should refer to Dostoevsky's disapproval of traditional Western ideas. p. 12*)

6. Discuss Marmeladov's self-analysis. (*The introduction of his character reveals his paradoxical nature. He acknowledges that he is a scoundrel who neglects his family, yet he will not accept responsibility for his own actions. He reveals that, by default, he has forced his daughter into prostitution, stolen from his wife, begged money from his daughter for liquor, and repeatedly lost jobs because of drinking. He proclaims his anguish for the misfortunes he causes his family, yet he declares that he drinks so he may suffer twice as much. He vows he deserves to be crucified, yet he wants others to pity him. pp. 13–21*)

7. Note the reference to the green shawl with which Sonia covers herself after her first night of prostitution. (*This is a family shawl that Sonia puts over her head and face as if to hide her shame. She then lies, shuddering, on the bed with her face to the wall [p. 16]. The shawl symbolizes suffering, as evidenced by the other times it is mentioned.*)

8. Discuss the introduction of the theme of religion, which will recur throughout the novel. Analyze the biblical allusions (p. 21) to God's forgiveness and the Image of the Beast: Luke 7:47, Revelation 13:16–17. (*Discussions will vary. Marmeladov is talking about Sonia, who has become a prostitute. He believes God will forgive her because she has loved much, just as God forgave the "sinner" woman in the Bible. He refers to himself as a swine, made in the Image of the Beast, but believes God will forgive him, and everyone, even Katerina, will understand all things. Inference*)

9. **Prediction:** What is Raskolnikov's "project," and will he be able to complete it?

Supplementary Activities

1. Working in small groups, have students prepare a job application and resumé for Marmeladov in his search for a new job.

2. Elicit student response concerning foreshadowing in the novel. Use the Foreshadowing Chart on page 6 of this guide to list examples of foreshadowing.

3. Literary Devices: **Similes**—he would creep down the stairs like a cat (p. 1); her thin long neck, which looked like a hen's leg (p. 4); his chin looked like a stiff greyish brush (p. 10).

Chapters III–IV, pp. 25–50

Raskolnikov receives a letter from his mother announcing the engagement of his sister, Dounia, to Luzhin and their impending arrival in St. Petersburg. Raskolnikov vows Dounia will not marry Luzhin.

Allusions: Bacchus (p. 29)—god of wine in Roman mythology; Golgotha (p. 39)—biblical reference in Matthew 27:33–35, literal meaning is the place of the skull, actual place is the hill on which Jesus Christ was crucified; Schilleresque (p. 41)—Schiller was a leading figure in German literature whose dramas feature pleas for human freedom and dignity; Jesuitical (p. 42)—Jesuits are members of a Roman Catholic religious order; Zeus (p. 43)—ruler of gods in Greek mythology

Vocabulary

monomaniacs (26)
expostulating (26)
ignominy (32)
infidelity (38)
malignant (38)
casuists (42)

Discussion Questions

1. Examine Raskolnikov's living conditions and what this signifies about him. (*He lives in a low-ceilinged, tiny room with peeling wallpaper and rickety furniture. Manuscripts and books covered with dust indicate he no longer attends school or gives lessons. His landlady, who threatens to go to the police because he will neither pay his rent nor leave, no longer provides his meals, and he subsists primarily on the few leftovers Nastasya provides for him. He can't even pay the postage due on a letter. He feels hopeless and longs for a fortune. pp. 25–27*)

2. Analyze the effect of Pulcheria's letter on Raskolnikov. (*Raskolnikov realizes he is the primary reason Dounia plans to marry Luzhin. He becomes intensely angry and vows the wedding will never be. He compares Dounia's sacrifice to the ascent to Golgotha, a place of suffering and death. He knows he must do something quickly if he is to prevent the marriage. pp. 28–40, 43–44*)

3. Discuss the nature of Sonia, Katerina Marmeladov, Pulcheria, and Dounia's suffering and what this says about the theme of suffering and gender in the novel. (*Discussions will vary. Note how each woman suffers for the sake of another—Sonia for her family, Katerina for her family, Pulcheria for her son, Dounia for her mother and brother. Raskolnikov's observance of his sister ascending to Golgotha by marrying a man she does not love for her brother's sake shows the parallel between suffering and sacrifice.*)

4. Examine Raskolnikov's comparison of Dounia's and Sonia's lives. (*He believes that, if Dounia marries Luzhin, she will be selling herself for her family just as Sonia sells herself in prostitution for her family. Luzhin would not love or respect her, just as Sonia's clients do not love or respect her. She would pay, as Sonia does, with bitterness and tears. pp. 40–43*)

5. Analyze the ambiguity of Raskolnikov's reaction to the plight of the drunken young girl he sees in the street. What does this say about his character? (*He gives a policeman money to see the girl home safely. Almost immediately, however, Raskolnikov changes his mind and tells the policeman to leave the girl alone. He rationalizes that it is none of his business what the man does to the girl and that she will very likely become a prostitute anyway. As he wavers between helping and ignoring the girl, he shows that he has two sides to his personality. pp. 45–49*)

6. Compare/contrast Raskolnikov and Razumihin. (*Both have attended the university, are poor, are intelligent, and have temporarily quit their studies. Raskolnikov views himself as superior to others and thinks their beliefs are beneath him; he is moody, unfriendly, temperamental, and has few friends. Razumihin treats everyone equally, is good-natured, sincere, and well liked. Raskolnikov is uninterested in returning to his studies; Razumihin is working hard to save enough money to return. Raskolnikov rarely drinks; Razumihin consumes a great deal of liquor. Raskolnikov is pessimistic about his future; Razumihin allows nothing to dampen his zest for life. pp. 49–50*)

Supplementary Activities

1. Have students write a diamente poem contrasting Raskolnikov and Razumihin.

2. Literary Devices: **Similes**—He had gotten away…like a tortoise in its shell (p. 26); letter had burst on him like a thunderclap (p. 44)

Chapters V–VII, pp. 50–83

Raskolnikov has a fearful dream of the death of an innocent horse. He goes to Alyona Ivanovna's apartment, where he kills both her and Lizaveta. He barely escapes undetected.

Allusions: Pushkin (p. 52)—considered Russia's greatest poet; Turgenev (p. 52)—one of Russia's greatest novelists

Vocabulary

ineradicable (61)
perpetuity (62)
ingenious (66)
stupefaction (76)
hapless (76)

Discussion Questions

1. Analyze Raskolnikov's dream. What point is Dostoevsky making by giving his characters dreams? (*As he contemplates the murder of Alyona Ivanovna, he dreams that he is a child walking with his father through the town of his birth. They pass a tavern, where they observe several drunken peasants torture and kill a horse. He runs to the bleeding horse and kisses its eyes and lips. Sobbing, he asks his father why the men killed the horse; his father replies they are drunk and brutal. Note that Raskolnikov's compassionate reaction to the horse's death foreshadows his eventual repentance. Raskolnikov awakens and realizes the dream reflects his own plan to kill the pawnbroker but rationalizes that he can never do it. Dostoevsky uses dreams to reflect the unconscious, psychological motivations in his characters. pp. 52–58*)

2. Examine the role of "chance" in Raskolnikov's decision to commit the murder. (*He walks through the Hay Market, even though he has no need to go there, where he overhears Lizaveta agree to visit a friend at 7:00 the following evening. He believes destiny has arranged for Alyona Ivanovna to be alone. In a previous casual conversation, Raskolnikov had learned of the pawnbroker and had gone to her and pawned something. After leaving Alyona's apartment, he overhears two young men discuss her cruelty and miserliness and allude to the possibility of killing her and using her money to aid the destitute. This trivial talk has convinced Raskolnikov that he is destined to kill her. After deciding to commit the murder, "chance" enables him to get the axe. He views these instances of "chance" as evidence of his superiority, i.e., fate makes it easier to perpetrate his crime. pp. 58–69*)

3. Examine Raskolnikov's actions and reactions during the crime and analyze his effectiveness as a criminal. Note the completion of the foreshadowing of the cigarette case on page 7 of the novel. (*He arrives at Alyona's apartment undetected, enters, and asks to pawn a silver cigarette case. As she questions him about it, he strikes her with the axe and kills her. While he is searching for money and retrieving various articles, Lizaveta comes in, sees her sister lying in a pool of blood, and then sees Raskolnikov. He murders her. Overcome with fear, he tries to get away but a visitor, Koch, rings the doorbell. He overhears Koch and another man implying that something is wrong. Koch stays while the other gets the porter. "Chance" intervenes when Koch leaves his post, enabling Raskolnikov to escape, and again when, after being spied, he is able to hide in an empty apartment. He returns to his room after replacing the axe. Effectiveness: He fails to close the door before committing the murder, yet has the presence of mind to wash the blood from the axe, his hands, and his boots. Raskolnikov is so intent on trying to maintain control mentally that he focuses on details while ignoring more obvious circumstances [e.g., the door being open], causing him to make mistakes even though he is trying to attend to every detail. pp. 72–83*)

4. Recall the conversation Raskolnikov overheard between a young man and an officer. Discuss the question, "would not one tiny crime be wiped out by thousands of good deeds"? (*Discussions will vary. Note the young man's emphasis on utilitarian values. p. 63*)

5. **Prediction:** Has Raskolnikov committed the "perfect murder"?

Supplementary Activities

1. Have students write a dialogue reflecting Raskolnikov's inward struggle before he commits murder.

2. Literary Devices: **Similes**—(the mare) fell on the ground like a log (p. 56); blood gushed as from an overturned glass (p. 74); The steps...like a dream in which one is being pursued (p. 78).

Part II, Chapters I–II, pp. 85–112

Raskolnikov, consumed with fear, hides and eventually disposes of the stolen articles. He is called to the police department for failure to pay his rent and faints when the murder is mentioned. He becomes ill.

Allusions: Noah's Ark (p. 101)—Bible, Genesis 6:14–22; Rousseau (p. 107)—French philosopher, important writer during Age of Reason

Vocabulary
cynicism (90)
affronted (93)
satire (96)
charlatanism (107)
enigmatic (109)
infinite (111)

Discussion Questions

1. Examine Raskolnikov's reactions the day after the murder and analyze the significance of these reactions. (*He thinks he's going mad. He becomes anxious, depressed, and paranoid, afraid he will betray himself by failing to hide the stolen items or by overlooking blood left on his clothing. He develops a fever, has chills, and becomes physically ill. From this point on, Raskolnikov's psychological torment increases as he wavers between his desire to confess and his desire to remain free. pp. 85–91*)

2. Discuss why Raskolnikov is called to the police department and analyze how he reacts. (*His landlady has filed charges against him for failure to pay his rent. When the summons comes, he is fearful that they know he has committed the murders, yet thinks they cannot possibly know. He reacts to his landlady's charges by becoming argumentative, disrespectful, and irrational, and by insulting the police official, Ilya Petrovitch. He is overcome with feelings of alienation from everyone and has a strong impulse to confess. He faints when he overhears a conversation about the murders he committed and leaves filled with terror, convinced that the police suspect him. Note that this chapter introduces police officials as specific antagonists. pp. 88–102*)

3. Discuss the internal conflict Raskolnikov experiences regarding whether or not to confess. How does this relate to the theme of freedom vs. slavery? (*Discussions will vary. Note that Raskolnikov's decision not to confess does not free him from punishment altogether, but that he continues to suffer psychologically and physically because of the crime he committed.*)

4. Analyze Raskolnikov's interaction with Ilya Petrovitch and Nikodim Fomitch and what this reveals about each of them. (*When he first begins to question Raskolnikov, Petrovitch looks at him suspiciously and indignantly, and Raskolnikov stares back heedlessly, thus insulting Petrovitch's "exalted" position. Raskolnikov responds to Petrovitch's shouts that he is late by angrily refuting the claim and telling Petrovitch that he allows no one to shout at him. They each accuse the other of being disrespectful. Raskolnikov addresses his explanation to Fomitch, who is agreeable, remains unperturbed, and tries to calm Petrovitch. Raskolnikov reveals his pride, Petrovitch his temper and desire to be respected, and Fomitch his composure and rationality. pp. 93–102*)

5. Examine Raskolnikov's actions when he returns from the police station and the irony of his actions. (*He retrieves the eight articles from their hiding place, puts everything in his pockets, and decides to throw them into the canal. He finally decides to bury the items under a large stone in a courtyard. After leaving the courtyard, he is distracted and vacillates between giddiness, somberness, and anger. He wonders why he didn't even look in the purse, then blames his actions on his illness. Only one day after the murders, his self-punishment intensifies, and he becomes sick of it all and begins to hate everything around him. He decides to visit Razumihin, but is rude and uncommunicative. He refuses work that Razumihin offers him and leaves. He takes a coin an old woman offers him but throws it in the river. He now feels totally isolated from everyone and everything. Ironically, he intended to use the money from the stolen items to help others, but because of his fear, they are now buried and are helpful to no one. pp. 102–106*)

6. Analyze Raskolnikov's dream about his landlady and what this signifies. (*In his dream, he awakens to horrible screams from his landlady and pleads with Ilya Petrovitch not to beat her. He hears a number of voices and loud noises and is terror-stricken, believing they will come for him next. Nastasya awakens him, brings him food, and tells him it is a dream and no one is beating the landlady. He is filled with anxiety when she comments, "It's the blood," until she explains it's the blood rushing to his head because of his weakness. The dream signifies Raskolnikov's guilt, his ensuing terror of being detected, and his fear of anyone he considers to be a pursuer. pp. 110–112*)

7. Discuss the symbolism of water in these chapters. (*Water symbolizes purity or cleansing. Note how Raskolnikov does not throw the stolen items in the canal, but rather buries them in the dirt. Also note how he falls into forgetfulness after swallowing and spilling water on his neck on page 112 of the novel.*)

8. **Prediction:** Will guilt cause Raskolnikov to confess?

Supplementary Activities

1. Working in small groups, have students do one of the following, then share their responses with the class: (a) research and correlate Raskolnikov's symptoms with those of a psychosomatic illness (b) write a five-senses poem about "Guilt" (c) write and stage a skit depicting Raskolnikov at the police department (d) write a newspaper article about the murders.

2. Literary Devices: **Similes**—(the confrontation) was something like a thunderstorm; she pattered...like peas dropping (p. 95); He felt as if a nail were being driven into his skull (p. 100); (Raskolnikov)...quivering like an over-driven horse; Terror gripped his heart like ice (p. 110).

Chapters III–V, pp. 112–145

Raskolnikov remains ill and delirious. He receives money from his mother. Zossimov, Nastasya, and Razumihin discuss the murder and the suspects.

Vocabulary
treacle (114)
capriciously (116)
metaphysical (118)
affectation (135)
brigands (139)
inveterate (143)

Discussion Questions

1. Discuss Raskolnikov's illness and what this time period reveals about Razumihin and Nastasya. (*For four days, Raskolnikov is semi-conscious and sometimes delirious. He does not remember the murders, yet he torments his mind. Throughout his illness, he realizes Nastasya and someone he cannot remember are at his bedside. He returns to complete*

consciousness just as a young man appears, bringing him money from his mother. Raskolnikov learns that Razumihin is the man who has tended to him faithfully throughout his illness, has brought Zossimov, a doctor, to see him, has retrieved the IOU from the landlady, and has brought him new clothes. Nastasya has fed him and cared for his needs during his illness. Razumihin and Nastasya are true friends who expect nothing in return. pp. 112–124)

2. Discuss Razumihin's references to personnel from the police department and the effect these have on Raskolnikov. (*Razumihin learns about Raskolnikov's affairs, including his impending eviction, while searching for him. He has become acquainted with police officials Fomitch and Ilya Petrovitch. He reveals that he and Zametov, the head clerk at the police department, have become friends, and he has brought Zametov to see Raskolnikov. Raskolnikov is filled with terror when he learns that Zametov heard him, during his delirium, rave about earrings, chains, an island, Fomitch, Petrovitch, his sock, and fringe from his trousers. After Razumihin and Nastasya leave, Raskolnikov frantically searches for and finds the trouser fringes, and his mental torment fills his mind with thoughts of escape. He drinks some beer and sinks into a deep sleep. pp. 119–121)*

3. Discuss the conversation about Razumihin's housewarming party and analyze how this advances the plot. (*In discussing the invited guests, Razumihin reveals that Zametov and Porfiry Petrovitch, head of the Investigation Department, will be there. This leads to a discussion of the murders. Razumihin is helping Zametov prove the innocence of the accused painter, who was implicated because of earrings he found in the apartment and later tried to sell. Raskolnikov realizes he must have dropped the earrings when he stepped inside the empty apartment after the murders. Razumihin discusses the reasons Nikolay could not possibly have committed the murders and gives the scenario just as Raskolnikov knows it happened. Raskolnikov is immobilized and silent during the discussion. pp. 125–134)*

4. Discuss Luzhin's arrival and his interaction with Raskolnikov. Analyze what this reveals about Luzhin, Raskolnikov, and Razumihin. Note the foreshadowing of Razumihin's relationship with Dounia. (*Luzhin displays his arrogance immediately as he scrutinizes the meager room furnishings and the disheveled and unkempt appearance of Raskolnikov and Razumihin. Luzhin is dressed meticulously in new clothes and obviously wants to give the impression of wealth and superiority. Razumihin is appalled when he learns of the lodgings Luzhin has arranged for Raskolnikov's mother and sister. Razumihin and Luzhin engage in a heated discussion about the rise of crime in people of higher social standing, the murder of the pawnbroker, and new philosophical ideas. Raskolnikov initially insults Luzhin with his apathy and disinterest. Raskolnikov becomes irate when talking about Luzhin's rationale for marrying Dounia and threatens him with bodily harm when Luzhin speaks derogatorily of Raskolnikov's mother. pp. 135–144)*

5. Analyze the aftermath of the conflict between Luzhin and Raskolnikov. (*Raskolnikov is highly agitated, accuses Razumihin and Zossimov of tormenting him, and demands that they leave him alone. He treats Nastasya rudely. Zossimov suggests that some fixed idea weighs heavily on Raskolnikov's mind and points out that the murder is the only thing in which he indicates any interest. Zossimov wants to delve into the psychology of Raskolnikov's actions. pp. 144–145)*

6. **Prediction:** Do Zossimov and Razumihin suspect that Raskolnikov is the murderer?

Supplementary Activities

1. Have students stage a grand jury investigation into the murder, ending in an indictment against Nikolay based on circumstantial evidence. Appoint a judge, district attorney, and members of the grand jury.

2. Literary Device: **Simile**—he turned as white as chalk (p. 130)

Chapters VI–VII, pp. 145–182

Raskolnikov and Zametov discuss the murder. Raskolnikov returns to the murder scene. Marmeladov dies after being run over by a carriage. Raskolnikov assists the family and meets Sonia. His mother and sister arrive in St. Petersburg.

Vocabulary
melancholy (152)
sacrament (172)
peremptorily (174)

Discussion Questions

1. Discuss Raskolnikov's actions after Razumihin and Zossimov leave. Analyze his conversation with Zametov. (*He immediately dresses in his new clothes and goes to the Hay Market. He feels strangely clearheaded and talkative and is enlivened by the singing, the dancing, and the women. He enters the Palais de Cristal [The Crystal Palace], where he meets Zametov. Raskolnikov initiates a conversation with him about the murders, during which he tells him he is reading the papers to find out more about the old woman's murder and implies that he knows a great deal about the crime. Zametov relates a psychological profile of the murderer, and Raskolnikov responds by telling Zametov how he would have behaved if he were the murderer. He proceeds to describe his own actions after the murders. Raskolnikov's desire to confess almost overpowers his desire to escape detection. He comes close to confessing but concludes their conversation by insinuating that he has been toying with Zametov's mind. He leaves, feeling exhilarated but extremely weary. Zametov concludes that Raskolnikov is strange but innocent of murder. pp. 145–156*)

2. Examine the conflict between Raskolnikov and Razumihin and the result. Contrast their personalities. (*Razumihin has been concerned about Raskolnikov and has been searching for him. Raskolnikov angrily tells Razumihin that he doesn't want his benevolence and to leave him alone. Razumihin initially reacts in an angry outburst but then invites him to his party. Raskolnikov refuses and leaves. Razumihin is concerned about Raskolnikov's mental state and searches for him but can't find him. Razumihin, a good-hearted man with a desire to seek truth and justice, is presented as a foil to Raskolnikov, who sought justice in society by committing a crime and is now self-absorbent and forced to lie to keep himself from being caught for his crime. Razumihin is offering Raskolnikov solace but is repeatedly rejected. pp. 156–160*)

3. Analyze why Raskolnikov returns to the murder scene and how he reacts there. (*Raskolnikov heads toward the police station with a strong inclination to confess but returns to the murder scene instead. He rings the bell just as he did the night of the murder, then engages in conversation with the workmen who are refurbishing the apartment. He tells them he is looking for an apartment and asks them leading questions about the women's blood left on the floor. He tells the workmen to come to the police station and he will tell them who he is. The custodians come and question him, then fling him into the street. This is the second time Raskolnikov almost confesses. Later in the novel, Porfiry Petrovitch reveals the suspicion aroused by Raskolnikov's actions at the Crystal Palace and the murder scene. Note the indications that Raskolnikov, through his impulsive actions, is his own worst enemy. pp. 160–164*)

4. Discuss Marmeladov's death. Analyze its effect on Raskolnikov and on Katerina. Discuss whether Katerina loves Marmeladov and what role she might have played in his downfall. (*Raskolnikov arrives on the scene just after Marmeladov is run over by a carriage. He assists the police in getting him to his apartment, offers to pay for a doctor, and later gives Katerina most of his money, signifying that he is not wholly cruel. This incident reveals Raskolnikov's compassion and his desire to atone for his own sin by helping someone else. When Marmeladov is brought into Katerina's presence, she quits complaining of her poverty because of him, drives the crowd away so*

he can die in peace, and sends Polenka for Sonia. Katerina reveals her bitterness toward her husband in her conversation with the priest, questioning what she must now do with the children, accusing Marmeladov of throwing himself under the horses, proclaiming that he was a drunkard, and thanking God that he is dying. Marmeladov tries to speak and ask her forgiveness. pp. 165–175)

5. Discuss the theme of religion and how it affects Raskolnikov after he leaves Marmeladov's family. (*Discussions will vary. After Marmeladov dies, Raskolnikov asks Polenka to pray for him and feels renewed strength. He feels a surge of freedom, though it is not clear that he truly feels repentant. He realizes that he did not die when he murdered the old woman. He decides not to confess and instead goes to Razumihin's party. pp. 176–177)*

6. Discuss the merging of the primary plot, Raskolnikov's crime, and the subplots involving Sonia and Dounia. (*Raskolnikov meets police captain Fomitch at Marmeladov's apartment, and he comments on the blood on Raskolnikov. His reply, "Yes...I'm covered with blood" has a double meaning: Marmeladov's blood and the symbolic blood of the women Raskolnikov killed. Razumihin later reveals to Raskolnikov that the police have suspected him of the murder but now attribute his actions to what Zossimov calls "madness." Sonia arrives, Marmeladov asks for her forgiveness, and he dies in her arms. After Raskolnikov leaves, he recalls seeing someone "with a flame-colored feather," foreshadowing Sonia's role in his future. Razumihin returns home with Raskolnikov, where his mother and sister are waiting for him. Razumihin's actions when Raskolnikov faints cause Dounia and her mother to view him as their "Providence," foreshadowing Razumihin's love and care for Dounia. pp. 175–182)*

7. Discuss why Raskolnikov faints upon seeing his mother and sister. (*Discussions will vary. p. 182)*

Supplementary Activities

1. Have students choose one of the emotions portrayed in this section (e.g., anger, bitterness, hopelessness, unforgiveness) and write a metaphor or simile poem about it.

2. Have students create a collage, using words and pictures, depicting Raskolnikov's many faces in the book thus far.

3. Literary Devices: **Similes**—her skirt inflated like a balloon over her back (p. 159); all was dead and silent like the stones on which he walked (p. 164); arms as thin as sticks (p. 176). **Metaphor**—Zossimov: piece of beef (p. 179)

Part III, Chapters I–III, pp. 183–220

Raskolnikov tells Dounia she must not marry Luzhin. Razumihin is romantically attracted to Dounia and assists her and her mother after Raskolnikov sends them away. Luzhin threatens to leave Dounia if he is forced to be in the presence of Raskolnikov.

Vocabulary
despot (185)
timorous (186)
homage (189)
juxtaposition (196)
dormouse (197)
hypochondria (198)
diffident (201)
sage (208)

Discussion Questions

1. Analyze the interaction of Raskolnikov, Dounia, Pulcheria, and Razumihin and what this reveals about each of them. Note the complication to the subplot involving Dounia's engagement. (*Pulcheria is distraught by Raskolnikov's irrational behavior toward her and Dounia and by his demand that Dounia break her engagement to Luzhin. Razumihin acts as a mediator*

between the three of them, attributes Raskolnikov's irritability to his illness, and offers to take care of him. Razumihin's infatuation for Dounia, including declarations of her beauty, an inventory of her admirable characteristics, his pledge of undying affection for her, and his jealousy toward Zossimov, add a lighter tone to the novel and complicate the subplot of Dounia's engagement. This section reflects Raskolnikov's continuing self-absorption and his insensitivity, e.g., the way he treats his mother and sister. He acts erratically due to his guilt and anxiety. Dounia remains calm and rational. Pulcheria reacts with motherly concern and anxiety. Razumihin is compassionate and honest. pp. 183–194)

2. Examine developments in the subplot concerning Dounia and Luzhin. (*After Razumihin sobers up, he regrets his impulsive behavior the day before, yet he dresses carefully and is eager to see Dounia again. He recants his previous negative remarks about Luzhin and criticizes Raskolnikov for insulting him. Razumihin reads a letter from Luzhin to Pulcheria in which he announces his intent to withdraw from the engagement if he has to meet Raskolnikov [as he disfavors Raskolnikov after their first meeting]. Dounia will not consent to this stipulation and asks Raskolnikov to be present at the next meeting with Luzhin. Dounia announces her intent to marry Luzhin to escape poverty. Another complication in the subplot arises with the announcement of the death of Svidrigaïlov's wife, Marfa Petrovna, foreshadowing the reappearance of Svidrigaïlov in Dounia's life. pp. 196–205, 217–220*)

3. Analyze Razumihin's summation of Raskolnikov and how his mother and sister react. Do you agree with Razumihin, or do you have another interpretation of Raskolnikov's actions? (*Razumihin tells Dounia and Pulcheria about some of Raskolnikov's recent actions. He then relates that Raskolnikov, whom he has known for a year and a half, alternates between two characters. He has always found him to be reserved, morose, and haughty, but has recently found him to be suspicious and introspective. He believes Raskolnikov has a noble, kind heart but can be cold and callous. Raskolnikov claims to be quite busy, yet he lies in bed and does nothing. He thinks highly of himself and isn't interested in what others do or say, and Razumihin thinks Raskolnikov does not love anyone and perhaps never will. Dounia thinks her brother needs a woman's care. Pulcheria thinks they are both mistaken because Raskolnikov has always been moody and capricious and does things no one else would think of doing, e.g., his engagement to the landlady's dying daughter, who was neither pretty nor rich. Responses will vary. pp. 200–202*)

4. Discuss Raskolnikov's continuing symptoms of mental aberration and analyze why he faints during his conversation with Dounia. (*When Dounia, Pulcheria, and Razumihin visit Raskolnikov the morning after his rude behavior, he is dressed and sitting up but is pale and listless and looks as if he has suffered some terrible physical torment. His face lights up briefly when he sees his mother and sister, but the light swiftly dies away. He apologizes for his previous behavior but is restless, speaks little, and is often confused and forgetful. He seems determined to endure their visit but has no joy in it. He becomes anxious and frightened by Zossimov's probing questions about the reasons for his illness. He tells them that he helped the Marmeladov family but can't explain his actions. This prompts a remark from Zossimov that a madman can be aware of his actions, yet his direction for those deeds can seem like a dream. Raskolnikov realizes this is true of his actions relating to the murder. He wavers between congeniality and irritability, asks why they are afraid of him, and mentally reflects on his hatred for them all. He erupts angrily when he confronts Dounia about her intent to marry Luzhin, yet vows she can marry whom she likes and agrees to accompany her to meet Luzhin if she wishes. When Dounia says, "I am not committing a murder," Raskolnikov faints because of the guilt he feels over his own crime. pp. 207–220*)

5. **Prediction:** What will happen when Luzhin meets Raskolnikov again? Will Dounia marry Luzhin?

Supplementary Activities

1. Have students write a diamente poem contrasting Pulcheria's two children: Raskolnikov and Dounia.

2. Literary Devices: **Similes**—He entered looking as black as night (p. 199); he turned as red as a crab (p. 201); It's (Raskolnikov's room) like a tomb (p. 216) **Metaphor**—Zossimov's possibilities with Raskolnikov's landlady: end of the world, anchorage, haven (p. 195)

Chapters IV–VI, pp. 220–259

Sonia brings Raskolnikov an invitation from Katerina to attend Marmeladov's funeral. Raskolnikov goes to ask Porfiry Petrovitch about items he had pawned and is convinced Petrovitch knows he is the murderer. Raskolnikov and Razumihin discuss the murder and Raskolnikov's article on crime. Svidrigaïlov comes to Raskolnikov's room.

Allusions: Romeo (p. 231); Kepler and Newton (p. 242)—German astronomer and mathematician whose laws of planetary motion Isaac Newton used to arrive at his theory of gravitation; New Jerusalem (p. 243)—Bible, Revelation 21:1–2; Lazarus rising from the dead (p. 244)—Bible, John 11:1–44; Lycurgus (p. 246)—Spartan legislator (800s B.C.); Mahomet (p. 246)—a.k.a. Muhammad, founder of Islam; Napoleon (p. 247)—crowned himself emperor of France; Waterloo (p. 255)—Napoleon's final battle, the defeat that ended Napoleon's political ambitions to rule Europe.

Vocabulary
calumny (221)
corpulence (233)
socialist (238)
phalanstery (239)
dissembler (240)
castigate (245)
ambiguous (250)
aesthetic (256)

Discussion Questions

1. Examine the interaction between Sonia and Raskolnikov. Elicit student response concerning the man who follows Sonia when she leaves Raskolnikov. *(While Pulcheria, Dounia, and Razumihin are present, Sonia, timid and shy, comes to his room to invite him to Marmeladov's funeral and the dinner following. She is now dressed modestly and poorly in contrast to her flashy prostitute's clothes of the day before. She is embarrassed and uncomfortable around the two ladies, but Raskolnikov introduces her and explains her father's death. Sonia is dismayed by Raskolnikov's poverty and realizes he gave her family everything he had. Pulcheria tries but is unable to greet Sonia. Dounia attentively and courteously bows to her. Although uneasy around Sonia, Raskolnikov is obviously drawn to her. Sonia feels that a new world is opening for her because of him. He agrees to come to the funeral. The man who follows Sonia is Svidrigaïlov, who has a room next to hers. pp. 219–228)*

2. Discuss why Raskolnikov asks Razumihin about Porfiry Petrovitch and the results of their visit to him. Note that Petrovitch becomes Raskolnikov's primary antagonist. *(Raskolnikov asks if Petrovich is responsible for investigating the murder. Razumihin, who is related to Petrovitch, takes Raskolnikov to Petrovitch's house to retrieve items Raskolnikov pawned to the old woman. Discussions about why Raskolnikov asks about Petrovitch will vary. Suggestions—Raskolnikov wants to retrieve his possessions; Raskolnikov wants to converse with Petrovitch to see if Petrovitch suspects him. When the two men visit Petrovitch, Raskolnikov tries to appear lighthearted, but he is filled with fear about what Petrovitch knows. His anxiety intensifies when he discovers that Zametov is also present. Raskolnikov and Petrovitch discuss the pawned items and then engage in a game of "cat and mouse," with each trying to outwit the other. The "game" leaves Raskolnikov*

feeling anxious and inadequate. He realizes Petrovitch knows the truth and struggles to keep his rage under control, fearing he will betray himself. He almost confesses and longs to tell the police investigators how he despises them. Petrovitch attempts, but fails, to trap Raskolnikov with his question about the painters. pp. 226–249)

3. Analyze the metaphor, "The butterfly flies to the light" (p. 230). (*Responses will vary. Raskolnikov is the butterfly, and Petrovitch is the light. Raskolnikov knows that Petrovitch is interested in him and that he is thorough in his investigations. Raskolnikov knows that, when he enters Petrovitch's house, the "light" of Petrovitch's insight may expose his dark secret. Inference)*

4. What themes appear in Raskolnikov's article, "On Crime," and how does it affect the book's plot? Note the "chance" incident. Discuss whether or not you agree with Raskolnikov's opinion. (*References to this article introduce some of the tenets of nihilism. Raskolnikov attests to his belief in God and says that the struggle between ordinary and extraordinary people will continue until the New Jerusalem, i.e., establishment of a new heaven and earth when Jesus Christ returns. He presents his idea that those who perpetrate a utilitarian crime will punish themselves with public acts of penitence and mental suffering. The article sheds light on the theme of religion, especially sin, repentance, and redemption, as well as the theme of nihilism vs. socialism. Razumihin is appalled at Raskolnikov's philosophy. Note that the allusion to Lazarus' rising from the dead foreshadows Raskolnikov's confession of his crime to Sonia and his eventual "resurrection." Chance: Petrovitch happened to find and read the article, alerting the readers to the fact that the murder investigator is aware of Raskolnikov's philosophy of crime. Responses will vary. pp. 240–249)*

5. Examine Raskolnikov's reaction to his meeting with Petrovitch. (*Through his discussion with Razumihin, Raskolnikov discovers that Petrovitch and Zametov have suspected him for some time. Razumihin assures Raskolnikov that they have no proof, or they would have arrested him. Raskolnikov angrily accuses Razumihin of wanting to torture him. Terror-stricken, he then rushes to assure himself that none of the evidence is left in the original hiding place. Finding no remaining evidence, he leaves and encounters a stranger who calls Raskolnikov a murderer. pp. 249–254)*

6. Analyze Raskolnikov's reflections on the murder. Discuss his rationale for murder. (*He believes that he did not kill a human being, but rather a principle. He believes the old woman is a louse, yet in his thoughts he admits to himself that perhaps he is a viler louse than the one he killed. He declares his hatred for the old woman and vows he will never forgive her. In this mental state, his hatred for his mother and sister reflect his guilt. He regrets killing Lizaveta and compares her to Sonia, who has given up everything for her family just as Lizaveta gave up everything for her sister. He falls into a nightmarish sleep during which he revisits the murder scene and attempts to kill the old woman, who laughs at him. This nightmare signifies his insecurity and concern about his inferiority. Responses will vary. pp. 255–256)*

7. **Prediction:** Who is the stranger who calls Raskolnikov a murderer? What does Svidrigaïlov's arrival portend for Raskolnikov?

Supplementary Activities

1. Have students research nihilism and participate in an oral discussion correlating their discoveries with Raskolnikov's ideas.

2. Literary Devices: **Similes**—You (Razumihin) are like a summer rose (p. 231); he swore he would squeeze Porfiry like a lemon (p. 252).

Part IV, Chapters I–III, pp. 261–292

Svidrigaïlov comes to ask for Raskolnikov's help in his search for Dounia and announces his plans to give her money. Raskolnikov learns from Razumihin that Petrovitch and Zametov suspect him. Dounia breaks her engagement to Luzhin. Raskolnikov leaves after telling his mother and sister he must remain apart from them.

Vocabulary
apoplexy (262)
propensity (264)
ingenuously (267)
benevolent (275)
pecuniary (277)
ephemeral (278)
conjugal (281)
fatuity (285)

Discussion Questions

1. Discuss Raskolnikov's meeting with Svidrigaïlov and the outcome. Note Svidrigaïlov's importance in Dounia's dilemma about Luzhin. (*Svidrigaïlov tries to justify his actions toward Dounia and denies having anything to do with his wife's death. He asks Raskolnikov to arrange a meeting for him with Dounia because he wants to warn her about Luzhin and give her money. When Raskolnikov refuses to allow Luzhin to see Dounia, Svidrigaïlov asks him to tell Dounia of an inheritance she will receive from Marfa Petrovna. This inheritance will provide financially for Dounia and Pulcheria and make it easier for Dounia to break her engagement with Luzhin. pp. 261–273*)

2. Examine Svidrigaïlov's explanation of his marriage to Marfa Petrovna. Evaluate the success of this type of marriage. (*He reveals that his wife bailed him out of prison for debts he owed due to gambling, and that she had held his IOU for a large sum of money until the previous year. He claims that they lived harmoniously, that he managed her estate wisely, and that he used a whip on her only two or three times. They had special arrangements concerning relationships with others. Responses will vary. pp. 263–266*)

3. Analyze the implications of Svidrigaïlov's experiences with ghosts. (*[1]Since his wife's death, she has "visited" him three times: first, to remind him to do something; second, to allude to something that will happen on his journey; and third, to taunt him about his prospects of a future marriage. [2] A servant, with whom Svidrigaïlov had quarreled violently, visited him after his death. Both "ghosts" come after unexplained deaths, suggesting Svidrigaïlov's implication in their deaths. Svidrigaïlov implies that he and Raskolnikov are similar. Note how Svidrigaïlov's visits from ghosts correlate with Raskolnikov's nightmare in which the pawnbroker still lives. pp. 266–269*)

4. Discuss the significance of Dounia's confrontation with Luzhin. Examine how this situation advances the plot. (*Luzhin is upset and almost leaves because Raskolnikov and Razumihin are present. He intends to punish Dounia and Pulcheria for disobeying him. At first Luzhin is congenial and attempts to ingratiate himself with Pulcheria by revealing information Marfa Petrovna had given him about Svidrigaïlov. Dounia reveals the strength of her character when she demands an explanation from Luzhin about his accusations against Raskolnikov. Luzhin reveals his true character when he refuses an explanation, demands her full allegiance to him, and refuses to be considered an equal of Raskolnikov. Pulcheria accuses Luzhin of falsely accusing Raskolnikov of giving money to Sonia, a prostitute. The confrontation ends when Dounia breaks the engagement. Luzhin leaves, mentally blaming Raskolnikov for everything. During the confrontation, Raskolnikov reveals information about Svidrigaïlov's visit and Dounia's inheritance from Marfa Petrovna. This section fills in details of earlier references by revealing details about Svidrigaïlov's marriage, his involvement and probable rape of a young girl who later committed suicide, and his cruel treatment leading to the death of the servant. Razumihin's irate response to Luzhin's insinuations that the earlier gossip about Dounia might be true foreshadows his desire to protect and love her. pp. 273–285*)

5. Discuss Luzhin's response to the broken engagement and analyze his character, e.g., his conceit and vindictiveness. (*He is astonished that Dounia would reject him and dismayed that she and her mother have escaped his control. He resolves to get her back, reflecting on her desirability, his belief that she must humble herself before him, and his vision of her charm and education helping him rise in prominence. Conceit: filled with self-admiration, including his appearance, his intelligence, and his wealth that makes him equal with his former superiors; justifies his actions and his lack of true love for Dounia. Vindictiveness: vows to crush Raskolnikov. pp. 285–288*)

6. Compare the characters of Luzhin and Raskolnikov. (*Responses will vary. Note both men's self-absorption and willingness to take advantage of another. However, note the difference in each man's ultimate goal in doing so.*)

7. Analyze Raskolnikov's conduct after Luzhin leaves. (*Dounia and Pulcheria respond enthusiastically to Razumihin's proposal of a business partnership for all four of them. When he realizes Razumihin's intent to take care of his mother and sister, Raskolnikov announces his departure and accidentally lets slip that he may never see them again. The impact of his crime and his desire to protect those he loves most drive him to leave. He asks Dounia and Pulcheria to let him go and forget him, indicating his concern for them instead of himself. His muttered words, "...I'm coming" indicate his intention to confess or his belief that he will soon be arrested. Razumihin follows him, and in their parting scene, he realizes the truth about Raskolnikov's crime. pp. 285–292*)

8. **Prediction:** What does Raskolnikov plan to do?

Supplementary Activities

1. Working in small groups, have students stage one of the scenes from this section: the meeting between Svidrigaïlov and Raskolnikov, the confrontation between Dounia and Luzhin, or the final scene between Raskolnikov and the others. The presentation can be recorded or live.

2. Literary Devices: **Similes**—rupture affected him like a clap of thunder (p. 286); a fever of excitement as though a ton-weight had fallen off his heart (p. 287)

Chapters IV–VI, pp. 292–333

Raskolnikov goes to Sonia's room and asks her to read him the story of Lazarus from the Bible. Raskolnikov goes to the police investigation department to retrieve his pawned items, and Porfiry Petrovitch engages him in a psychological mind game. Nikolay confesses to the murders.

Allusions: Sevastopol, Alma (p. 315)—city and river where important battles of the Crimean War were fought; Gogol (p. 329)—major Russian playwright who wrote a satire, *The Inspector-General*, about corruption among government officials.

Vocabulary
ironical (314)
allegorical (318)
imperiously (323)
punchinello (324)

Discussion Questions

1. Discuss why Raskolnikov goes to Sonia's room and analyze their conversation. Note the merging of the primary plot with a subplot. (*Responses will vary. Suggestions: Raskolnikov believes he can find comfort and strength from Sonia, a "sinner" who is destroying her own life, and he desires to understand how an honorable and a dishonorable nature can exist side-by-side. Their*

conversation reveals Sonia's love and sense of responsibility for Katerina, who is now mentally deranged and approaching death, and her children. Sonia talks of deep faith in God and her belief in His divine care. The plots merge when Raskolnikov learns of Sonia's friendship with Lizaveta and sees the New Testament and cross Lizaveta gave Sonia. Raskolnikov's paradoxical behavior confuses and frightens Sonia when he becomes harsh, rejects her faith, and accuses her of being unhinged, then almost immediately kneels and kisses her foot, saying he bows down to all the suffering of humanity. He eventually asks her to go away with him, and, before he leaves, says he will tell her who killed Lizaveta if he comes again. pp. 292–308)

2. Discuss why Raskolnikov asks Sonia to read the story of Lazarus and what the story signifies to both of them. (*Responses will vary. To Sonia, the story symbolizes her desire to rise from her life of poverty, abuse, and shame and her faith that she, too, will experience the glory of God's resurrection power from her old life to a new one. Although Raskolnikov denies belief in the Bible, the story offers a glimmer of hope that he can find forgiveness for his terrible sin and start a new life. This scene also foreshadows the day when both Sonia and Raskolnikov will be "resurrected" from their old lives and find a new beginning. pp. 292–308)*

3. What does Svidrigaïlov's eavesdropping indicate? (*Responses will vary. Note his plans to make himself more comfortable the next time he listens through the door, foreshadowing his eventual discovery of Raskolnikov's guilt. p. 308)*

4. Analyze Porfiry Petrovitch's interrogation of Raskolnikov. (*Raskolnikov goes to the police station to take his written request for the pawned watch to Porfiry Petrovitch. He hates having to see Petrovitch again and fears the encounter. Petrovitch treats him cordially, but Raskolnikov feels that Petrovitch is leading him into a trap. Petrovitch has no solid proof that Raskolnikov is the murderer, but he attempts to manipulate him into a confession. Raskolnikov confronts Petrovitch and demands that he either examine him properly or let him go. Petrovitch switches his tactics and engages in idle chatter, then teasingly presents some ideas about investigating a criminal. The two engage in another psychological mind game, with Petrovitch probing and Raskolnikov trying to remain calm and refusing to respond. Raskolnikov finally erupts in fury, proclaiming that he knows Petrovitch thinks he killed the two women but saying he refuses to allow Petrovitch to torment him. Petrovitch tells Raskolnikov that he knows all about him, including his visit to the murder scene. Petrovitch becomes conciliatory and seems concerned about Raskolnikov's health but soon alludes to a surprise. At the climatic point of the interrogation, Nikolay bursts into the room and confesses to the murders. pp. 308–325)*

5. Discuss how Petrovitch and Raskolnikov react to Nikolay's confession. Why do you think Nikolay confesses? What eases Raskolnikov's mind after leaving the police department? (*Petrovitch does not believe Nikolay is the murderer but questions him about details. He tells Raskolnikov to leave but cautions him that they will meet again. Raskolnikov realizes how close he came to confessing. Responses will vary. As Raskolnikov leaves, the man who had previously called him a murderer tells him that he observed him come to the murder scene and ask about the blood and has reported his actions to Petrovitch. He now believes he has falsely implicated Raskolnikov and asks for forgiveness. pp. 325–333)*

6. When the man who accused Raskolnikov asks for forgiveness, Raskolnikov replies, "May God forgive you" (p. 332). Why doesn't Raskolnikov offer his own forgiveness? Do you think Raskolnikov believes in God's forgiveness? If so, discuss what actions a person must take to receive such forgiveness, according to Raskolnikov. (*Responses will vary.*)

7. **Prediction:** Will Nikolay be convicted?

Supplementary Activities

1. Have students make an acrostic for "Resurrection" based on Sonia's hopes.

2. Literary Devices: **Similes**—(Sonia's hand) transparent, like a dead hand (p. 294); (Raskolnikov) looked like a madman (p. 299); I shake with laughter like an india-rubber ball (p. 312); The temperament reflects everything like a mirror (p. 318).

Part V, Chapters I–III, pp. 335–375

Luzhin and Lebeziatnikov discuss nihilism. Luzhin gives Sonia money for Katerina, then accuses her of stealing. Katerina's funeral dinner for Marmeladov turns into a fiasco. Lebeziatnikov comes to Sonia's defense.

Allusions: Fourier (p. 338)—important French socialist; Darwinian theory (p. 338)—theory of evolution; Raphael (p. 344)—influential painter of Italian Renaissance, famous for gentle paintings of the Madonna and Child; Pushkin (p. 344)—considered Russia's greatest poet, author of a novel in verse about an intelligent, good-hearted character who destroys himself and others because he lacks moral discipline and purpose in life

Vocabulary
parsimony (337)
nihilists (337)
scrofulous (338)
beggarly (339)
indecorous (346)
subscription (347)
provincial (355)
vouchsafe (357)
burgomeister (361)
pettifogging (365)
commiserating (367)
harangue (370)
impunity (374)

Discussion Questions

1. Examine evidence of Luzhin's true character. (*He is selfish and materialistic and becomes angry and frustrated with anyone who opposes him. He decides his stinginess is the source of his problems with Dounia. He shows his vindictiveness and deceit when he gives Sonia money on the pretense of helping Katerina and the children. He is actually setting her up by slipping a large bank note into her pocket in order to accuse her of stealing from him. pp. 335–336, 344–350*)

2. Discuss the relationship between Luzhin and Lebeziatnikov and note the merging of the subplots. (*Luzhin originally thought Lebeziatnikov, who is a nihilist, could help him learn about the progressive thinking of the younger generation in St. Petersburg. When Lebeziatnikov fails to inspire him, Luzhin comes to despise and fear him. Lebeziatnikov dislikes Luzhin and has learned that he is not the "right sort of man."*

   Plots: Lebeziatnikov lives in the same rooming house as the Marmeladovs; he, Luzhin, and Raskolnikov are invited to the funeral dinner where Sonia will be present. pp. 337–339)

3. Analyze Dostoevsky's portrayal of Lebeziatnikov. (*Through his portrayal of Lebeziatnikov, Dostoevsky criticizes the perspective of nihilism, i.e., the rejection of established beliefs that became popular in Russia in the middle 1800s. Lebeziatnikov is a contradictory character who, though he expounds a progressive doctrine, is actually rather uneducated and commonplace. He, for some unexplained reason, had beaten Katerina, yet he comes to Sonia's defense against Luzhin's false accusations. He declares his belief that prostitution is normal and says he respects Sonia for using her "assets" and assuming this lifestyle, yet it is rumored that he is the one who had her removed from the building. He believes he has helped in Sonia's development, yet he has not asked her to join his "community" because he sees no place for prostitutes in that community. He vows his respect for her chaste modesty around him, yet he secretly hopes she will desire him. pp. 337–344, 368–369*)

4. Discuss the funeral dinner, i.e., Katerina's rationale for hosting it, the elaborate preparations, the guests, and her reactions to everyone. (*Rationale: pride, e.g., her need to prove that Marmeladov was in no way inferior to anyone and to demonstrate her ability to entertain properly; guilt, e.g., her references to the way she treated him. Preparations: Although destitute, she spends half the money she received from Raskolnikov on the dinner, which includes liquor and several types of food. Guests: primarily the poorest and most insignificant of those invited; the older and more respectable do not come; Katerina is pleased when Raskolnikov arrives because he is educated. Reactions: She begins to taunt her landlady, Amalia Ivanovna, whom she blames for the lack of respectable guests. The two women erupt into shouting verbal insults. After Luzhin's accusations of Sonia are proven false, the guests attempt to detain Luzhin, and the dinner ends in a melee. Amalia Ivanovna commands Katerina to leave her lodgings at once. pp. 350–361, 373–374*)

5. Analyze Luzhin's conspiracy against Sonia, including his motive and the outcome. Note the author's use of "chance" to enhance the plot. (*He plans to confront Sonia at the funeral dinner and "prove" that she stole the money from him. In an attempt to prove Sonia's innocence, Katerina tells Sonia to turn out her pockets, and the bank note falls out. Motive: Luzhin hates Raskolnikov, whom he blames for his problems with Dounia, and intends to embarrass him by accusing Sonia. Outcome: Lebeziatnikov accuses Luzhin of slander and declares that he saw him slip the money into Sonia's pocket. Raskolnikov explains Luzhin's desire for revenge against him. Luzhin leaves, threatening to prosecute Sonia. He does not appear in the novel again. Chance: Lebeziatnikov happens to see Luzhin slip the money into Sonia's pocket and to arrive at Katerina's just in time to testify to this fact, proving Sonia's innocence. pp. 362–374*)

6. **Prediction:** Why is Raskolnikov going to see Sonia?

Supplementary Activities

1. Have students (a) draw a caricature of Lebeziatnikov or (b) write a name poem for him.

2. Literary Devices: **Similes**—she (Katerina)…held her as in a vice (p. 365); landlady waved her away like a feather (p. 374) **Metaphors**—Luzhin's wounded vanity: black snake (p. 335); the landlady: an owl, a Prussian hen's leg (pp. 358, 365)

Chapters IV–V, pp. 375–404

Raskolnikov confesses to Sonia and later learns that Svidrigaïlov overheard his confession. Katerina dies.

Allusion: Punch and Judy show (p. 398)—comic puppet shows with rough, violent humor that were popular in England

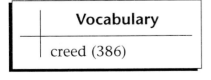

Vocabulary

creed (386)

Discussion Questions

1. Analyze Raskolnikov's compulsion to confess his crime to Sonia and her reaction to the confession. Note Sonia's role as a Christ figure, offering hope and redemption for Raskolnikov. (*After his intense defense of Sonia against Luzhin's accusations, Raskolnikov feels that he must fulfill his word to her and reveal who killed Lizaveta. He views Sonia as a fellow sinner and believes they have both sinned for the right reasons; e.g., she to aid her family; he to rid the world of a "louse." He alludes to his earlier statement that they must go on the same road together [p. 307]. By confessing to Sonia, he hopes to alleviate some of his guilt and find forgiveness. After his confession, Sonia is filled with compassion and tells him*

she will follow him anywhere, even to Siberia [foreshadowing his eventual punishment]. Sonia begs him to repent and declares that only through suffering can he atone for his sin. She offers to give him her [literal] cross and to bear the [figurative] cross with him. Raskolnikov begins to open his heart to Sonia's love. Although not yet willing to confess to the police and accept his punishment, he implies that he will eventually do so. He later feels completely alone and is remorseful because he believes he has poisoned Sonia's life. pp. 375–391, 393)

2. Examine Raskolnikov's rationale and primary motivation for murdering the pawnbroker. Analyze his allusion to Napoleon. (*He tells Sonia that he killed because he wanted to become a Napoleon, i.e., to exert his own superiority, to dare to transgress the law, and to control his own fate. He confesses that he killed for himself alone because he wanted to see if he was a man or a louse, only to discover that he is a louse like all the rest because he now feels guilt. He says he did not kill for money or to help anyone, yet acknowledges the pressure he felt because his mother's and sister's hopes centered on him. Although he admits murder was wrong, he justifies his actions by blaming the deaths on the devil and saying he only killed a "louse." In retrospect, he declares that he murdered himself, not the old woman, thus crushing himself once and for all. Responses will vary. pp. 383–389)*

3. Discuss why Lebeziatnikov comes to Sonia and how the ensuing events advance the plot. (*He informs Sonia that Katerina has gone out of her mind after being cast out, and possibly beaten, while attempting to find help for herself and her children. She is shouting and beating the children, vowing to take them to the streets to beg because everyone has abandoned her. Raskolnikov, Sonia, and Lebeziatnikov leave to search for Katerina. Lebeziatnikov's arrival interrupts the intensity of Raskolnikov's confession. It sets the stage for the climax and denouement of the Marmeladov subplot, which is complete when Svidrigaïlov pays for Katerina's funeral and provides funds for the children's care. Sonia remains an important character in the main plot of Raskolnikov's "crime and punishment." Svidrigaïlov's revelation that he has overheard Raskolnikov's confession to Sonia signals the "beginning of the end" of the primary plot. pp. 391–404)*

4. Examine Dounia's visit to Raskolnikov. (*She comes to tell him she has heard of the suspicion and persecution by the police and reveals her love and concern for him. Raskolnikov, who is seriously contemplating a confession to the police, hints that this is his final farewell to her. He assures her of Razumihin's good character and capability of real love, hinting at a future relationship between Dounia and Razumihin. He is tempted to confess to her but believes her incapable of accepting such news. pp. 393–394)*

5. Apply the adage "Pride goes before destruction" to Katerina Marmeladov's decline. (*Her pride and dignity, which have sustained her through poverty and illness, is destroyed when her father's former associates reject her. She is left with nothing to cling to and resorts to begging, which is, in her opinion, the lowest form of life. Even though she is dying from consumption, she vigorously coaxes and coerces her children to beg. In response to Sonia's and Raskolnikov's pleas to return home, she launches into a monologue that reveals her madness and loss of hope. Her sense of pride returns briefly when she refers to her aristocratic family. Her frenzied outburst ends when she loses consciousness, and a policeman takes her to Sonia's apartment, where she dies. pp. 395–403)*

6. Analyze Katerina's deathbed statement, "I have no sins..." (p. 402). (*She rejects the idea of a priest to absolve her of her sins because she believes God must forgive her of all sins because of the intense suffering she has experienced in her life. Because of her assumed martyr syndrome, Katerina believes she has atoned for her sins and that God will find no fault in her. Inference)*

7. **Prediction:** How will Svidrigaïlov use his knowledge of Raskolnikov's guilt?

Supplementary Activities

1. As a class, write a metaphor or simile about revenge, remorse, compassion, and pride.

2. Literary Devices: **Similes**—(Sonia) started as though she had been stabbed (p. 380); They sat...as though they had been cast up by the tempest alone on some deserted shore (p. 390).

Part VI, Chapters I–II, pp. 405–427

Raskolnikov's mental torment about the murder is intensified by Porfiry Petrovitch's visit. Petrovitch confronts Raskolnikov with his suspicions and tries to persuade him to confess.

Allusion: Seek and ye shall find (p. 424)—Bible, Matthew 7:8.

Vocabulary

tacitly (406)
self-abnegation (407)
pernicious (414)
mitigation (424)
bourgeois (424)

Discussion Questions

1. Examine Raskolnikov's actions following Katerina's death and Svidrigaïlov's revelation. Discuss Razumihin's visit, noting the reference to a mysterious letter Dounia has received. (*Raskolnikov feels as if he is in a fog. He wanders about aimlessly, and his emotions range from panic to apathy as he attempts to escape reality. He worries about what Svidrigaïlov will do now that he knows Raskolnikov is the murderer. Svidrigaïlov slyly alludes to the crime, but the two never actually discuss it. Razumihin comes to check on Raskolnikov and alludes to a letter Dounia has received from Svidrigaïlov that hints at some crime Raskolnikov has committed [pp. 410–412, 449–452]. Raskolnikov reacts by telling Razumihin of his conversation with Dounia about Razumihin. Razumihin mentions the murder and implies that Petrovitch believes Nikolay to be the murderer. Raskolnikov leaves to confront Svidrigaïlov but discovers Petrovitch in the hallway. pp. 405–414*)

2. Analyze the "mind game" between Porfiry Petrovitch and Raskolnikov, i.e., Petrovitch's investigative tactics and Raskolnikov's response. (*Petrovitch appears at Raskolnikov's room unexpectedly and begins to engage in idle chatter and later praises Raskolnikov's noble character. His countenance varies from friendly smiles to serious, sad expressions. He mentions their previous meeting and apologizes for acting unfairly, then keeps Raskolnikov wondering about his real purpose. Petrovitch implies that he thinks Raskolnikov is innocent, yet he refers to the actions of a guilty person and relates Raskolnikov's own actions, e.g., his fainting spell at the police station when the murder was mentioned; his anger and boldness in the restaurant with Zametov; the visit to and bell ringing in the apartment where the murder occurred. He then reveals that he does not believe Nikolay is guilty, and that the portrayal of the murderer fits Raskolnikov, not Nikolay. Raskolnikov realizes from the beginning that Petrovitch is playing professional tricks on him. He responds to Petrovitch by greeting him without flinching, yet his voice falters when discussing Nikolay, and his lip twitches throughout their conversation. He scornfully accuses Petrovitch of being up to his old tricks, denies that he is the murderer, and reminds Petrovitch that he, Raskolnikov, has admitted nothing. pp. 414–427*)

3. Examine Petrovitch's parting words. How do you think Raskolnikov internally responds to Petrovitch's final words? (*He paints a bleak picture for Raskolnikov's future and tells him that he is convinced he will ultimately confess because he will choose to suffer. Petrovitch refers to a providential "fact" he has that will prove Raskolnikov's guilt, then offers to help him and tells him his sentence will be lessened by a voluntary confession. In his final admonition, Petrovitch*

tells him to leave a note if he chooses to commit suicide. Responses will vary. Note Raskolnikov's irritation and impatience after Petrovitch leaves. pp. 423–427)

4. Analyze why Nikolay confesses to the murders. (*He is childish, innocent, easily influenced, and feels guilty because of earlier thievery. He became religiously fervent under the spiritual guidance of the elder of a religious sect for two years. When he arrived in St. Petersburg, he forgot his religious teaching and participated in a life of women and wine. Thinking they suspected him of the murders, he ran away and tried to hang himself. After being put in prison, he remembered his religious teaching, especially dwelling on the spiritual application and benefits of suffering. Petrovitch suspects that Nikolay now wants to suffer but thinks he will recant his confession. pp. 420–421)*

5. **Prediction:** Where is Raskolnikov going and why?

Supplementary Activities

1. Have volunteers stage the mind game between Petrovitch and Raskolnikov, noting especially the body language.

2. Literary Devices: **Similes**—it was as though a fog had fallen upon him (p. 405); chase and capture you like a hare (p. 422)

Chapters III–V, pp. 427–459

Raskolnikov meets Svidrigaïlov in a tavern. Svidrigaïlov reveals his debauchery and later attempts to seduce Dounia.

Vocabulary
obsequious (430)
vice (434)
swinishness (437)
profligate (437)
epithet (442)
debauchery (445)
blackguard (449)

Discussion Questions

1. Discuss the role of "chance" in Raskolnikov's meeting with Svidrigaïlov and examine their conversation. (*After Petrovitch leaves, Raskolnikov wavers between going to Svidrigaïlov or to Sonia. He decides to go see Svidrigaïlov but inadvertently detours through the Hay Market, where he happens to see Svidrigaïlov in a tavern. As they converse, Svidrigaïlov reveals information about his life and credits Dounia with trying to save him. Raskolnikov threatens to harm him if he attempts to use his knowledge of Raskolnikov's confession to get to Dounia. Svidrigaïlov denies his plans to entice Dounia and tells Raskolnikov of his engagement to a young girl. He insinuates that he will keep silent about Raskolnikov and will soon depart. pp. 428–445)*

2. Analyze Svidrigaïlov, based on what he reveals to Raskolnikov. Note the foreshadowing of his suicide on page 435 of the novel. (*He is complex and paradoxical. His generosity to the Marmeladov family covers his hidden motive of becoming involved with Raskolnikov because of Dounia. He discusses his debauchery, but alludes to his faithful adherence to a contract with his wife. He reveals his questionable past, including the death of a child and a servant. He proclaims his love and respect for Dounia, yet later attempts to rape her. He acknowledges his fear of death, yet later commits suicide. He pretends not to have understood details of Raskolnikov's confession to Sonia, then alludes to his murdering the old woman. He portrays himself as sensual, devious, and manipulative. pp. 432–446)*

3. Discuss Svidrigaïlov's meeting with Dounia: why she agrees to meet him, his behavior, and her response. Analyze what this reveals about both of them. (*Dounia meets Svidrigaïlov at the bridge because of his letter alluding to Raskolnikov's part in a crime. He tricks her into going to his apartment with him by mentioning Raskolnikov's crime and telling her Sonia will confirm the*

confession. When she realizes the rooms are secluded, Dounia is frightened, uneasy, and distressed; Svidrigaïlov is condescending and excited. Dounia lays the letter on the table, says she has heard but does not believe the rumors, and reminds Svidrigaïlov of his promise to prove his allegations. Svidrigaïlov relates details of the confession, and Dounia almost faints when she realizes he has lied about Sonia's arrival. She attempts to leave, but the door is locked. He proclaims his love for her. Dounia realizes he intends to rape her and commands him to open the door. He tries to get her to submit to him by threats against Raskolnikov and Pulcheria. Dounia takes a gun from her pocket, accuses him of killing his wife, and fires two shots; one grazes his head and the other misfires. Svidrigaïlov taunts her to shoot again, but Dounia drops the revolver and begs him to let her go. Svidrigaïlov, knowing he cannot control himself for long, tells her to "make haste," then allows her to leave because he realizes she will never love him. Dounia's reaction signifies her inability to harm another person even if the act is justified. His retrieval of the gun foreshadows his suicide. Responses will vary. pp. 449–459)

Supplementary Activities

1. Write a name poem for Svidrigaïlov based on his self-analysis.

2. Literary Devices: **Similes**—It was a strange face, like a mask...(p. 432); (Svidrigaïlov's fiancée) flushing like a sunset; face is like Raphael's Madonna (p. 443) **Metaphors**—Dounia: bird flying into a cage (p. 439); Svidrigaïlov's fiancée: an unopened bud (p. 443)

Chapters VI–VIII, pp. 460–490

Svidrigaïlov visits Sonia and later commits suicide. Raskolnikov goes to his mother, then, after telling Dounia of his plans, he confesses.

Allusions: Achilles (p. 471)—a figure in Greek mythology, the greatest Greek warrior in the Trojan War; taking up cross (p. 482), drink the cup (p. 486)—Bible, Mark 8:34, Matthew 26:39, both refer to Christian symbolism of suffering

Vocabulary
perturbation (462)
lachrymose (484)

Discussion Questions

1. Analyze the climax of the Svidrigaïlov subplot, i.e., his suicide and the significance of this subplot to the story. Note the symbolism of the weather. (*After Dounia rejects Svidrigaïlov, he spends the evening roaming around, then goes to his flat where he gets money and tears up some papers. He goes to Sonia and tells her he might be going to America, gives her money for herself, and assures her of his provision for the Marmeladov children. He then visits his fiancée's home, tells the family of his impending departure, and gives them a large amount of money. About midnight, he takes a room in a dirty, rat-infested hotel. He becomes feverish, begins to reflect on Dounia, and is haunted by a series of mental images. He drops off to sleep and has a nightmare about a small, neglected child whom he rescues, only to have her become an image of depravity. He awakens at 5:00 a.m., writes a few lines in a notebook, walks toward the river, and shoots himself. Responses will vary regarding the importance of the subplot to the story. Note how Svidrigaïlov's presence created tension in the novel as he both knew of Raskolnikov's crime and had the power to manipulate Dounia, though she resisted his manipulations. The presence of his character allowed the author to shed light on others' characters. Note the paradox: Svidrigaïlov, who is depraved by his lust for women, provides a way for Sonia to escape her life of prostitution. Weather: dark, stifling, threatening storm clouds erupting into downpour, roaring wind; morning of suicide: cold, damp, thick mist. The raging storm symbolizes the storm within Svidrigaïlov. pp. 460–472*)

2. Examine why Raskolnikov goes to see his mother and the universality of her reactions. Note the significance of his appearance. (*His appearance signifies his inward conflict: he is soaking wet, dirty, and ragged; his face is distorted by fatigue and exposure. He knows this will be his final visit to his mother because he intends to confess. He wants her to assure him of her undying love regardless of what happens to him or what she hears about him. Pulcheria welcomes him with tears and expresses her concern for him. She refers to reading his article and expresses her pride in him. She believes he will become one of the leading thinkers in Russia. She intuitively knows he faces great sorrow and tells him she will never believe anything bad about him. He tells her good-bye and asks her to pray for him. Raskolnikov's heart is softened by his mother's love. Universality: Pulcheria's unconditional love for her son, her pride in his accomplishments, her unwillingness to believe anything bad about him, and her faith in his future; Raskolnikov's need of a mother's unconditional love. pp. 472–476*)

3. Discuss Raskolnikov's confession to Dounia and her reaction. (*She comes to his room after waiting with Sonia all day for him. He admits that he considered suicide, but his pride prevented it. He tells her of his plans to confess but still alleges he did not commit a crime by killing a noxious insect and becomes furious when she mentions atoning for his crime. He begins to think he is a coward to confess but tells her he will try to be honest and act like a man. They leave together but later separate, signifying their destiny to go in different directions. Raskolnikov wishes he had never loved or been loved. pp. 477–481*)

4. Examine Sonia's importance to Raskolnikov regarding his confession. (*He had first confessed to her. She has promised to go with him wherever fate sends him, and her love and compassion comfort him. Before going to the police station, he comes for her cross, symbolizing his first step toward renewing his faith. He believes he has come to Sonia because of her tears rather than the cross. He asks Sonia not to go with him to the police station, then detours to the Hay Market, symbolizing his desire to escape and return to a degraded lifestyle. He sees Sonia watching him and realizes he has reached his "cross-road." As Sonia had suggested, he falls to the earth weeping and kisses the ground [pp. 388–389] but cannot bring himself to publicly confess as a murderer. He then goes to the police station but decides not to confess. As he is leaving, Sonia is again watching him. He returns and confesses to Ilya Petrovitch. pp. 481–490*)

5. **Prediction:** What sentence will Raskolnikov receive?

Supplementary Activities

1. Working with a partner, have students prepare a video recording of Raskolnikov's confession and the ensuing interrogation.

2. Literary Devices: **Similes**—I've become more particular, like an animal (p. 466); profile of her face looked as though chiseled of marble (p. 468); Raskolnikov felt as though something had fallen on him (p. 489) **Metaphors**—prison: water; Raskolnikov: stone (p. 481)

Epilogue, Chapters I–II, pp. 491–505

Raskolnikov is sentenced to eight years in prison. Sonia accompanies him to Siberia. Dounia and Razumihin marry, and Pulcheria dies. Raskolnikov feels he has been resurrected into a new life.

Vocabulary

conflagrations (502)

Discussion Questions

1. Examine the report of the trial and why Raskolnikov receives a relatively light sentence. (*Raskolnikov confesses and explains the crime in detail. He says he killed to improve the conditions of his life and doesn't try to justify himself. He attributes his confession to heartfelt repentance. He receives a light sentence of eight years partly because Zossimov testifies about his neurotic illness and Razumihin about his charitable deeds when a student. The lawyers and judges are impressed because he has not spent the money or used the stolen items, and they decide he committed the crime while temporarily insane. pp. 491–493*)

2. Discuss the denouement and whether or not the book ends as expected. (*Raskolnikov is in prison in Siberia. Sonia has accompanied him there and is well loved and respected by everyone, including the other prisoners. Razumihin has returned to school and anticipates a brilliant future. He and Dounia are married and hope to save enough money to settle in Siberia in a few years and begin a new life with Raskolnikov and Sonia. Pulcheria suspects the truth but never questions the story that her son is away on a business venture. She dies shortly after preparing for his return. pp. 491–496*)

3. Discuss Raskolnikov's reaction to prison and whether or not he repents of his crime. (*He is sullen, non-communicative, uninterested in most news from home, and basically unaffected by his mother's death. He accepts the crowded, miserable prison conditions and does his work but is disliked by other prisoners because of his air of superiority. He initially shows no true repentance and continues to mentally justify the pawnbroker's death, realizing it was a crime but feeling no remorse. He feels unsuccessful and hopeless, thinks his crime was in confessing, and wonders why he didn't kill himself. His pride and shame initially cause him to treat Sonia contemptuously and ultimately make him ill. pp. 497–501*)

4. Analyze the turning point in Raskolnikov's repentance/redemption. (*His dream of microbes attacking and almost destroying the human race awakens him to the danger of placing his faith in his own, or any human's, superiority. After the dream, he views everyone, including Sonia, differently. He has seen Sonia's unconditional love, her self–sacrificial nature, and her persistent faith, even when he has treated her contemptuously. He falls at her feet, and both of them feel renewed and happy. Her love and faithfulness spark hope in him that he, too, can be redeemed. He experiences an awakening of religious faith, e.g., his response to Sonia's cross and the New Testament, and he is ready to face the future with her. pp. 501–505*)

5. Analyze the themes of alienation, suffering, sacrifice, and redemption/resurrection in this section. (*Alienation: Raskolnikov's literal isolation in Siberia and his emotional and mental isolation from everyone. Suffering: Raskolnikov's mental and physical suffering in prison; Sonia's mental suffering because of Raskolnikov's contempt. Sacrifice: Sonia's sacrifice for Raskolnikov. Redemption/resurrection: Both of them have experienced a resurrection, she from prostitution, he from hopelessness; love is the key in both. Inference*)

Supplementary Activities

1. Have students bring to class newspaper or magazine articles involving a plea of temporary insanity in a criminal trial.

2. Have students write a diamente poem contrasting Raskolnikov before and after his "redemption."

Post-reading Discussion Questions

1. Using the Character Chart on page 7 of this guide, indicate an incident or time in the novel when each character experienced each feeling. Add other emotions as necessary.

2. Using the Characters with Character chart on page 8 of this guide, evaluate characters in the novel.

3. Using the Plot Chart on page 35 of this guide, analyze the plot development of the primary plot, Raskolnikov's crime and punishment, and the subplots involving Marmeladov (including Sonia) and Dounia (including Luzhin, Svidrigaïlov, and Razumihin). (*Suggestions—St. Petersburg is the setting for each plot. Raskolnikov—Problem: murders the pawnbroker. Events: plans and perpetrates the crime; lives in terror of being detected and psychologically punishes himself, his mother, and his sister; Porfiry Petrovitch interrogates him; he confesses the crime to Sonia. Climax: confesses the crime to Ilya Petrovitch. Resolution: is sent to prison in Siberia where he eventually finds redemption. Marmeladov—Problem: his alcoholism and its effect, e.g., his family's destitution, Sonia's prostitution, and his self-abnegation. Events: meets Raskolnikov, explains his problem, and takes him home with him, where Raskolnikov meets Sonia; Marmeladov dies; Katerina forces the children to beg. Climax: Katerina dies. Resolution: Svidrigaïlov provides financial assistance and Sonia is freed from prostitution.*)

4. Using the Story Map on page 9 of this guide, examine the components of the novel.

5. Discuss the sequence of events in Raskolnikov's journey from crime to punishment to repentance and redemption.

6. Analyze the symbolism of the Hay Market, Sonia's yellow ticket, the green shawl, and the story of Lazarus. (*The Hay Market is the poor area of St. Petersburg: symbolizes the dissolute lifestyle. Sonia's yellow ticket marks her as a prostitute: symbolizes Marmeladov's complete degradation and Sonia's shame, but also her love for her family. The green shawl symbolizes suffering. The story of Lazarus tells how Jesus raised Lazarus from the dead: symbolizes Sonia's hope that one can rise from sin to new life.*)

7. Analyze the development of themes in the novel, especially guilt/conscience, alienation, sacrifice, suffering, and redemption/resurrection. (*Responses will vary. Suggestions: Guilt/conscience: Raskolnikov suffers physically and mentally after committing murder. Even though he tries to justify himself, he ultimately must confess or lose his mind and his soul. Alienation: Raskolnikov's crime alienates him from everyone; Marmeladov's alcoholism alienates him from his family and society; Sonia's prostitution alienates her from society and drives her away from her family. Sacrifice: Sonia sacrifices her virtue for her family; Dounia is willing to sacrifice herself for her family. Suffering: Many of the characters suffer because of poverty; Marmeladov's family suffers because of his alcoholism; Sonia suffers rejection as a prostitute. Redemption/ resurrection: Both Sonia and Raskolnikov find peace and love and the chance for a new life.*)

8. Examine the importance of some of the minor characters. (*Responses will vary. Suggestions: Lizaveta: the innocent victim of Raskolnikov's plan. His conscience cannot justify her death as it does with Alyona Ivanovna. Nastasya: her care for Raskolnikov exemplifies unselfishness. Nikolay: the painter who confesses to the murders; adds suspense to the plot. Lebeziatnikov: portrays the nihilist philosophy in Russia in the mid-1800s; provides a solution to Sonia's problem with Luzhin.*)

9. Discuss the appropriateness of the title *Crime and Punishment*. What was Raskolnikov's true punishment after committing the murders—the period of time before or after confessing?

10. Analyze why Dostoevsky ends the novel with the inference to great striving and suffering in the future. What lies ahead for Raskolnikov and Sonia?

11. Discuss what the novel says about Dostoevsky's personality, political views, and religious views. What was he trying to communicate to his audience?

12. Discuss the distinctions made between males and females and the rich and poor throughout the book. How does Dostoevsky characterize different genders and social classes?

Plot Chart

Climax

Event # 3

Event # 2

Event # 1

Problem

Setting

Resolution

Post-reading Extension Activities

Note: For Writing Activity #1, distribute the Persuasive Writing Worksheet on page 10 of this guide to students.

Writing

1. Working in small groups, write a letter to the editor of your local newspaper stating your position, either for or against capital punishment.

2. Write a letter from Raskolnikov to Dounia following his "redemption."

3. Write a eulogy for either Marmeladov or his wife.

4. Tell Sonia's story in a ballad or narrative poem.

Art

5. Create a collage depicting Raskolnikov's journey from crime to redemption.

6. Design a poster advertising a movie about the novel.

Multi-Media

7. Working in a small group, write and stage a series of short vignettes featuring the most dramatic scenes from the drama. Present the scenes to the class on video, accompanied by appropriate background music.

8. Working in a small group, find pictures of nineteenth-century and modern-day St. Petersburg and Siberia, Russia. Prepare a slide show of pictures showing scenes in both locations. Write a narrative to accompany the pictures. Suggestion: Use a scanner or digital camera to obtain the pictures from still photographs, then prepare the slide show with a digital camera or computer.

Current Events

9. Bring to class newspaper clippings or magazine articles about life in present-day St. Petersburg.

10. Research and give an oral report about present-day prison conditions in Siberia.

Viewing

11. View one of the movies based on *Crime and Punishment*. Give an oral report to the class in which you discuss the similarities and differences between the novel and the movie. (Three movies have been produced based on *Crime and Punishment*: 1935, 88 min., 1958 [French], 108 min., updated version set in Paris, renamed *The Most Dangerous Sin*; 1959, 78 min., updated version featuring George Hamilton as a law student who becomes involved in robbery and murder.)

12. Present to the class selected clips from one of the *Crime and Punishment* movies. Discuss how the clip is similar to or different from the written version.

Assessment for *Crime and Punishment*

Assessment is an ongoing process. The following ten items can be completed during the novel study. Once finished, the student and teacher will check the work. Points may be added to indicate the level of understanding.

Name _____ Date _____

Student   **Teacher**

_____   _____   1. Write three review questions over the novel. Participate in an oral review.

_____   _____   2. Prepare and present to the class a charade depicting one scene from the novel that depicts one of the novel's major themes.

_____   _____   3. Correct all quizzes over the novel.

_____   _____   4. Display or perform your extension project on the assigned day.

_____   _____   5. Compose a chart detailing the symbolism incorporated throughout the novel.

_____   _____   6. Working in a small group, compare your completed character charts, story maps, and comprehension activities.

_____   _____   7. Write a poem about one of the major characters in the book. The poem should speak to the changes that occur in the character throughout the novel.

_____   _____   8. Write a review of the novel for the school newspaper. Use at least 12 of the vocabulary words.

_____   _____   9. Give at least one example for each type of conflict found in the novel: person vs. self, person vs. person, person vs. society. Write a paragraph explaining how each conflict is resolved.

_____   _____   10. Write an opinion paper in support of or refuting Raskolnikov's article, "On Crime," referred to in Part III, Chapter V.

Glossary

Part I, Chapters I–II, pp. 1–25
1. axiom (2): a well-established principle; self-evident truth
2. languid (11): not brisk or lively; sluggish
3. magnanimous (13): noble in soul or mind; generous
4. consumption (13): tuberculosis; a disease that destroys part of the body, especially the lungs

Chapters III–IV, pp. 25–50
1. monomaniacs (26): people whose behavior is characterized by monomania, a mental disorder in which they are obsessed or controlled by a single idea or emotion
2. expostulating (26): reasoning earnestly with a person; remonstrating in a friendly way
3. ignominy (32): public shame and disgrace; dishonor
4. infidelity (38): lack of religious faith; unbelief in Christianity
5. malignant (38): very evil; malicious
6. casuists (42): people who decide questions of right or wrong in regard to conscience or conduct

Chapters V–VII, pp. 50–83
1. ineradicable (61): cannot be rooted out or gotten rid of
2. perpetuity (62): forever, continuity, endlessness
3. ingenious (66): cleverly planned and made
4. stupefaction (76): dazed or senseless condition; stupor
5. hapless (76): unlucky; unfortunate

Part II, Chapters I–II, pp. 85–112
1. cynicism (90): act of doubting the sincerity and goodness of others
2. affronted (93): insulted; offended
3. satire (96): a poem, essay, or story that uses mockery or irony to attack or ridicule something
4. charlatanism (107): practice of quackery or pretending to have more knowledge or skill than a person actually has
5. enigmatic (109): puzzling; baffling; mysterious
6. infinite (111): endless; limitless

Chapters III–V, pp. 112–145
1. treacle (114): excessive sentimentality
2. capriciously (116): changing suddenly without reason
3. metaphysical (118): highly abstract; hard to understand
4. affectation (135): artificial way of talking or acting; pretense
5. brigands (139): people who use lawless methods to get what they want
6. inveterate (143): firmly established

Chapters VI–VII, pp. 145–182
1. melancholy (152): sadness; dejection
2. sacrament (172): communion; the consecrated bread and wine of the communion
3. peremptorily (174): allowing no denial or refusal; in a dictatorial manner

Part III, Chapters I–III, pp. 183–220
1. despot (185): a person who does just as he likes; tyrant; oppressor
2. timorous (186): easily frightened; terrified
3. homage (189): respect; honor
4. juxtaposition (196): placing side by side
5. dormouse (197): a small animal that sleeps most of the winter

6. hypochondria (198): abnormal anxiety over one's health; low spirits without any real reason; neurosis
7. diffident (201): timid, bashful; lacking self-confidence
8. sage (208): wise; using good judgment

Chapters IV–VI, pp. 220–259
1. calumny (221): false statements made to slander someone; defamation
2. corpulence (233): fatness; obesity
3. socialist (238): a person who favors socialism, a system or social organization by which the primary means of production and distribution are controlled by the government
4. phalanstery (239): a socialistic community
5. dissembler (240): a person who practices deceit; hypocrite
6. castigate (245): criticize; rebuke severely
7. ambiguous (250): having more than one possible meaning; doubtful; uncertain
8. aesthetic (256): having an appreciation of beauty; tasteful

Part IV, Chapters I–III, pp. 261–292
1. apoplexy (262): stroke; sudden loss or lessening of power to move
2. propensity (264): natural inclination
3. ingenuously (267): frankly; openly; sincerely
4. benevolent (275): desiring to promote happiness of others; charitable
5. pecuniary (277): having to do with money
6. ephemeral (278): lasting only a very short time; fleeting
7. conjugal (281): having to do with marriage
8. fatuity (285): self-satisfied stupidity; silliness

Chapters IV–VI, pp. 292–333
1. ironical (314): expressing one thing and meaning another; contrary to what would be expected; mocking
2. allegorical (318): explaining or teaching something by a story
3. imperiously (323): arrogantly; haughtily
4. punchinello (324): grotesque or absurd person

Part V, Chapters I–III, pp. 335–375
1. parsimony (337): stinginess; selfishness
2. nihilists (337): people who reject established beliefs or deny all existence
3. scrofulous (338): having to do with a form of tuberculosis characterized by enlargement of lymph glands and inflammation of joints
4. beggarly (339): mean; sordid; destitute
5. indecorous (346): not in accordance with proper behavior; disgraceful
6. subscription (347): a sum of money raised by several persons; fund
7. provincial (355): unsophisticated; lacking refinement
8. vouchsafe (357): to be willing to grant or give; bestow
9. burgomeister (361): mayor of a town
10. pettifogging (365): shifty; tricky; quibbling
11. commiserating (367): feeling or expressing sorrow for another's suffering
12. harangue (370): noisy speech
13. impunity (374): freedom from punishment or other consequences; exemption

Chapters IV–V, pp. 375–404
1. creed (386): any statement of belief or opinion

Part VI, Chapters I–II, pp. 405–427

1. tacitly (406): implicitly; by inference
2. self-abnegation (407): self-denial
3. pernicious (414): deadly; harmful
4. mitigation (424): process of making less severe; alleviation
5. bourgeois (424): characteristic of the middle class; ordinary

Chapters III–V, pp. 427–459

1. obsequious (430): polite or obedient from hope of gain; compliant
2. vice (434): an evil, immoral, or wicked act
3. swinishness (437): selfishness; greediness
4. profligate (437): very wicked, degenerate person
5. epithet (442): a word or phrase used in place of a person's name, often insulting or contemptuous
6. debauchery (445): excessive indulgence in sensual pleasure; dissipation
7. blackguard (449): a low, contemptible man

Chapters VI–VIII, pp. 460–490

1. perturbation (462): state of being disturbed or agitated
2. lachrymose (484): tearful; mournful

Epilogue, Chapters I–II, pp. 491–505

1. conflagrations (502): big, destructive fires